The GAMBOLS

BOOK Nº 45
by Barry Appleby

Pedigree® BOOKS

Published by Pedigree Books Ltd
The Old Rectory, Matford Lane, Exeter, Devon, EX2 4PS
Under licence from Express Newspapers plc.
Printed in Italy. ISBN 1.874507.67.8

£6.99

GA 45

Photo courtesy of Express Newspapers Group

Barry Appleby began his prestigious newspaper career as a journalist, producing a small trickle of articles out of an office on Fleet Street. His secretary at this time was the woman he would later marry and eventually team up with to produce the wealth of Gambols strips that have appeared since 1950.

Guided by Percy V Bradshaw of the Press Art School, Barry Appleby studied life at Heatherleys, design at the Victoria and Albert, anatomy at the Royal Academy, and commercial art at St Martin's. Long before his studies were completed however, he had discovered that the work he liked and sold quickest were cartoons, and very soon the first Barry Appleby drawings began to appear in *Punch*.

Barry and his wife, Dobs, began their commercial partnership before the Gambols were born, with a series of pocket sports cartoons in the *Daily Express*. Once their "pocket" was established, they approached the newspaper's Editor with their new creation, a strip called the Gambols. The Editor agreed to start using it three days a week. It had an immediate success, and the Gambols appeared more and more regularly until, from June 4th 1951, they appeared every day.

Each strip is a merging of ideas from Barry and Dobs. Once the idea was born, it was entered into their "gag-book" in the form of brief notes and a quick pencil sketch from Barry. A reference number and the date the cartoon was to appear in the newspaper were added later.

When Barry and Dobs were satisfied they had squeezed the utmost out of the idea, Dobs drew the "frames" or borders, after which Barry took over and pencilled the figurework and general composition. Then Dobs had another turn, this time pencilling the lines for the lettering. Back again to Barry, who put in the finished lettering and inked-in the figures. By mutual agreement Dobs became responsible for all feminine details, the backgrounds and domestic settings. The final touch, however, was Barry's prerogative … the signature.

Strikingly resemblant of George and Gaye in temperament, and even appearance, people who knew them would say if you knew the Gambols, you knew the Applebys. Barry and Dobs always denied it!

This book celebrates the lives of the Applebys and the Gambols. A collection of the best of the last twelve months strip is followed by a retrospective of the earliest cartoons.

Barry Appleby died in March 1996.

THE GAMBOLS by Barry Appleby

THIS IS VERY WELL PROCESSED GAYE—

YOU'RE VERY GOOD— I DON'T KNOW WHAT WE'D DO WITHOUT YOU

DO YOU MIND IF MY HUSBAND HEARS THIS?

© 1995 Barry Appleby
19-9 TUES 6482

THE GAMBOLS by Barry Appleby

NOW I'VE FORGOTTEN WHAT I WAS LOOKING FOR

© 1995 Barry Appleby
20-9 WED 6483

THE GAMBOLS by Barry Appleby

READ IT BACK TO ME GAYE—EXACTLY AS 1 DICTATED IT

EXACTLY AS YOU DICTATED IT...?

YES

© 1995 Barry Appleby

PERFECT

21-9 THURS 6484

NICE MAN

YES, VERY

DEDICATED

ABSOLUTELY

IN FACT THE ONLY MAN ON THE STAFF WITHOUT AN ULCER

TUES 2·4 6650

YOUR LETTERS, SIR

IS THIS ALL?

ER....YES...

....EXCEPT FOR ONE INTERESTING PERSONAL LETTER

3·4 WED 6651

CONGRATULATIONS GAYE

HUH?

YOU'VE JUST FOUND A SEVENTH WAY OF SPELLING 'EXPLICITLY'

THURS 6652

THE CHIEF ACCOUNTANT HAS BEEN WAITING TO SEE YOU – SIR

What's he want?

I DON'T KNOW

BUT FROM THE LOOK OF HIM – IT'S TROUBLE

SNIFF

FINAL ACCOUNT

©1996 Barry Appleby

19-4
FRI
6665

NO – I'M SORRY..

SHE CAN'T COME AND TALK TO YOU AT THE MOMENT...

SHE'S BEEN TRYING OUT A NEW RECIPE FOR A GIN AND BRANDY UPSIDE DOWN CAKE

©1996 Barry Appleby

20-4
SAT
6666

D.I.Y INCOME TAX

CLAIM

LATER

LATER STILL

YOU'VE BEEN AT THOSE FIGURES LONG ENOUGH DARLING

D.I.Y INCOME TAX

©1996 Barry Appleby

22-4
MON
6667

AN HOUR LATER

TWO HOURS LATER

AS I WAS SAYING

©1996 Barry Appleby

26-4
FRI
6671

GEORGE DEAR....

THAT REMINDS ME......

...DID YOU RENEW YOUR INSURANCE?

27-4
SAT
6672

I ALWAYS THOUGHT THAT IF I GOT A JOB.....

... AND INCREASE OUR INCOME—WE WOULDN'T HAVE TO WORRY ABOUT MONEY

OPTIMIST

©1996 Barry Appleby

29-4
MON
6673

I'LL ANSWER THE REST AFTER LUNCH

ah well — obviously he's not so young as he used to be

CHAIR

18·6
TUES
6716

© 1996
Barry Appleby

LOOK GEORGE..

I DON'T CARE WHAT HAPPENED AT THE OFFICE TO·DAY...

© 1996
Barry Appleby

JUST DON'T TAKE IT OUT ON ME

19·6
WED
6717

WHAT DO YOU MEAN ?...

SLAM
CHAIR

YOU'RE WAITING TO SEE HIM WHEN HE'S IN A GOOD MOOD ?

THIS IS HIS GOOD MOOD

CHAIRMAN

GROWL

20·6
THURS
6718

YOU KNOW THAT TO·DAY IS THE LONGEST DAY OF THE YEAR?

YES

SILVER POLISH

AND IT CERTAINLY SEEMS LIKE IT

JOBS STILL TO BE DONE

21·6 FRI. 6719

WHY DON'T YOU COOK IT IN THE KITCHEN?

NO!

IT WOULDN'T TASTE THE SAME

SISS

©1996 Barry Appleby

22·6 SAT 6720

HULLO PHYLIS

HI! JACKIE

'MORNING LOUISE

WOW! am I glad that I didn't manage to get to that sale

©1996 Barry Appleby

24·6 MON 6721

"**March 16th, 1950 – an outstanding date in the life of the Gambols. For on this day, George and Gaye Gambol made their first appearance as a strip cartoon in the *Daily Express*. Since then they have become real people to the millions of real people who follow their adventures with sincere affection. Every day, as the readers of the *Daily Express* go about their business, at home and at work, they see themselves mirrored in the human touches that bring the Gambols so close to them.**"

With these words began the Gambols first birthday book, and over the next pages, we take a look at some of the earliest Gambols' strips.

Barry Appleby once said, "We attempt to portray the funny little things that occur in every well regulated family. It's all a matter of recognising the fun when we see it, and our ability to laugh at ourselves".

Such was the appeal of even the earliest Gambols' cartoons, there is a little bit of every married couple in George and Gaye.

Let's take a look at the Gambols' early years …

LAST WEEK | BILL ASKED ME IF WE'D LIKE TO GO WITH HIM AND HIS WIFE ON A FISHING HOLIDAY — SHOULD BE FUN — FRESH FISH TO EAT

MONDAY | HULLO, IS THAT THE FISHMONGER?

DINNER

SUPPER

TUESDAY

WEDNESDAY

TO-DAY | NO, THANKS BILL, I CAN'T STAND THE SIGHT OF FISH THESE DAYS

WELL, IT'S VERY NICE TO HAVE YOU TO STAY WITH US AGAIN FLIVVER. HAVE YOU LEARNED TO BE A GOOD BOY? | YES

ALWAYS KIND AND THOUGHTFUL TO DUMB ANIMALS? | YES

LATER | HE FOLLOWED ME HOME | WELL, TAKE HIM AWAY AND LOSE HIM AGAIN

BUT THAT WOULDN'T BE BEING KIND AND THOUGHTFUL TO DUMB ANIMALS

Whenever Flivver leaves after a stay with the Gambols we receive dozens of letters, particularly from children, asking us to 'please make Flivver come back.'

What is Cocoa Slop?

*Here are some of the enquiries
made about this intriguing dish*

A nine-year-old Lancashire boy:

" I would like to taste that cocoa slop that you made for Flivver and Miggy this morning but my Mummy does not know how to make it so would you please send me the recipe."

A canteen manageress in South London:

" What is this stuff called ' cocoa slop' ? I have consulted various cookery books but cannot find anything approaching it. How exactly is it made, and how is it eaten (or drunk) ? "

A Durham housewife:

" My family of four were quite put out when I confessed that I didn't know how to make cocoa slop. This is what comes of being regular readers of the Gambols. For the sake of my prestige and peace and quiet, will you please send me the full details as soon as possible."

A telegram from a Devon hotel:

VISITOR SUGGESTS COCOA SLOP FOR MENU STOP COMPLETELY BAFFLED STOP PLEASE ENLIGHTEN

Recipe for COCOA SLOP

Ingredients

Two thick slices of bread
Two tablespoonfuls of cocoa
Two tablespoonfuls of sugar
Half a pint of milk or more if desired

Method

Cut bread into small squares and place in a dish, add the sugar and cocoa. Mix well. Heat the milk and pour over mixture and serve while still hot. Sufficient for one person

Time

Simmer for ten minutes

Oh dear! The trouble that ' cocoa-slop' caused. I should think that half the children in the country asked their mothers to make them some and nobody had ever heard of it. However, a few days later we gave the recipe. But not a single cocoa manufacturer ever wrote to thank us !

12

GAYE, I'VE GOT OLD JACK SONKIN AND HIS WIFE WITH ME — JUST MET THEM AS I WAS GOING TO THE STATION — THEY'RE PASSING THROUGH ON THEIR WAY UP NORTH — I'VE TOLD THEM THAT YOU'LL BE MOST UPSET IF I DON'T BRING THEM HOME WITH ME FOR THE NIGHT

TRRRIN-ING

LOOK! A FLY HAS SETTLED ON IT

I'LL GET IT OFF WHEN THE PAINT'S DRY

147

I'VE LOST ALL INTEREST IN SPRING CLEANING SINCE YOU DECIDED TO LEAVE ME

DON'T PUT IT LIKE THAT

I'M GOING TO PHONE THE DECORATORS TO-DAY AND TELL THEM TO FINISH THE JOB

MY HUSBAND STARTED ON THE JOB HIMSELF BUT I'VE PERSUADED HIM TO HAVE IT DONE PROPERLY

LATER ER... MY WIFE STARTED THE JOB HERSELF BUT... ER.. I'VE DECIDED IT WOULD BE TOO MUCH FOR HER

YES MR GAMBOL — SHE TOLD ME

9-3

COEE! DEAR! I'M HOME

WHEEE

WHAT HAPPENED?

HAVE YOU FORGOTTEN DEAR? FLIVVER AND MIGGY ARRIVED TO DAY

20·8

I MUST GO AND UNPACK
SHALL I COME AND HELP YOU?

YOU'VE BROUGHT A LOT OF SUITCASES WITH YOU, MIGGY

DID YOU WANT ALL THOSE CLOTHES?
OH THEY'RE NOT ALL CLOTHES

I COULDN'T LEAVE MY FAMILY AT HOME
22·8

WHAT ARE YOU DOING, AUNTIE GAYE?
SHELLING PEAS FOR DINNER

BUT MUMMY'S PEAS ALWAYS COME IN A PACKET

THESE ARE FRESH ONES

ISN'T THAT WONDERFUL?
WHATEVER WILL THEY THINK OF NEXT?
23·8

... AND I'VE NEVER SEEN ANYONE SO STRONG AS THAT MAN WHO TORE UP THE TELEPHONE DIRECTORIES

PHOO, I CAN DO THAT

THERE! NOW I'LL SHOW YOU HOW IT'S DONE

FIRST YOU TEAR ALL THE INSIDE PAGES AND LEAVE THE COVER INTACT SO THAT YOU CAN'T SEE WHERE IT'S BEEN TORN — LIKE THIS

LATER ... AND YOU MEAN TO SIT THERE AND TELL ME THAT YOU TORE THE TELEPHONE DIRECTORY IN HALF TO SHOW THEM A TRICK?

YES DEAR

POOLS

24-8

WELL, JUST ONE TO SEAL OUR BARGAIN

BAR

GOOD NIGHT AND I'LL SEND YOU A LETTER CONFIRMING THE ORDER TO-MORROW

BAR

COEE, GAYE, I'M HOME — HULLO YOU TWO

25-8

UNCLE GEORGE IS HOME AUNTIE

AND HE SMELLS JUST LIKE CHRISTMAS PUDDING

CAN WE BUY SOME NUTS FOR THE MONKEYS?

PLEASE UNCLE

LIONS →

NUTS

AREN'T YOU GOING TO FEED THEM, DEAR?

WE HAVEN'T ANY NUTS

WE'VE EATEN THEM ALL OURSELVES

27-8

THIS IS THE WAY THE RED INDIANS LIGHT THEIR FIRES

HALF AN HOUR LATER

I'LL GO AND FETCH SOME MORE DRY SHAVINGS — YOU CARRY ON RUBBING — IT JUST NEEDS PATIENCE

OH GOOD, YOU GOT IT TO BURN — IT JUST NEEDED PATIENCE

YES UNCLE

2-9

FAIR

SHY

DODGEMS

BIG WHEEL

7

ROLL 'EM

RIDES

TOMBOLA

WHIP

NO MORE, GEORGE, THEY'RE ONLY LITTLE CHILDREN, THEY'LL BE TIRED OUT

BUT THEY MUST SEE THE ZOO

CIRCUS

LION TIGE

LATER

WHAT SHALL WE DO NEXT?

CAND FOS

ICE

LITTER

3-9

ICES

FISH TEAS

CANDY FLO

CAN I HAVE ANOTHER CAKE, AUNTIE?

NO, DEAR

OH, LET THEM, GAYE, THEN THEY WON'T NEED ANY SUPPER WHEN THEY GET HOME

MEA 410

BUT WE HAVEN'T HAD ANY SUPPER — WE'LL STARVE DURING THE NIGHT

YOU'LL FIND SKELETONS IN THE BED IN THE MORNING

4-9

ASK THAT WOMAN IN FRONT OF YOU TO REMOVE HER HAT, DEAR

BUT I CAN SEE PERFECTLY

THAT ISN'T THE POINT

2B-9

ISN'T IT A LOVELY HAT DARLING?
UH HUH

IT'S *JUST* WHAT I'VE BEEN LOOKING FOR

IT'LL GO WITH MY...ER... NO.. I THINK I'LL GO BACK AND CHANGE IT FOR THE BLUE ONE

PIERR

*Well, that **must** be an all-time world record for change of mind*

1-10

ES, IT FITS VERY WELL, DEAR

I'LL WEAR IT TO THE OFFICE TO-DAY

WHERE'S MY WALLET AND MY POUCH AND PIPE?

26-10

MRS. LEAF'S HUSBAND'S UP NORTH ON BUSINESS AND HE'S HAD AN ACCIDENT

OH DEAR

I'M RUNNING HER UP THERE IN THE CAR.

GOOD IDEA

WILL YOU BE ALL RIGHT FOR A FEW DAYS?

OF COURSE

NOW I'LL BE ABLE TO DO **JUST** AS I LIKE

EVEN WASH UP WITHOUT WEARING MY APRON

WHILE GAYE'S AWAY I CAN HAVE A **REAL** NIGHT OUT

I'LL CALL AT THE OLD CLUB AND HAVE A DRINK OR TWO WITH THE BOYS

IT'LL BE LIKE THE DAYS BEFORE I MARRIED

...AND JOE GROUND?

OH, HE'S MARRIED TOO, WE NEVER SEE HIM HERE

...AND BILL ROCKERY?

HE MOVED DOWN SOUTH

NINE O'CLOCK

GOSH, HOW I MISS GAYE—I FEEL SO **LONELY** ON MY OWN

BUT THERE'S **ONE** THING I'VE ALWAYS WANTED TO DO **ALL** MY MARRIED LIFE

NOW'S MY CHANCE

GAYE! IF YOU THINK I'M GOING TO GET UP OUT OF THIS CHAIR AND WASH UP, YOU'RE CRAZY

MONDAY

TUESDAY

WEDNESDAY

STORE

PAPER PLATES

LAST WEEK

GAYE! ISN'T IT READY YET?

I'VE BEEN WAITING TEN MINUTES FOR MY BREAKFAST

SORRY, DEAR

TO-DAY

I'LL GRAB SOME BREAKFAST ON THE WAY TO WORK

AND YOU'LL HAVE TO WAIT ANOTHER TEN MINUTES

ALL THIS CLEANING TO DO AFTER THE MESS I MADE WHILE GAYE WAS AWAY

POOR GAYE... SHE'LL BE TIRED

GAYE, SHALL I TAKE YOU OUT TO DINNER?

OH, NO THANK YOU, IT'S TOO NICE TO BE HOME AGAIN

WE often receive letters from readers criticising Gaye for being empty-headed and only thinking of clothes. They ask why doesn't she belong to a club and occupy her time usefully.

But she does. She is often shown helping her club.

Even so, Gaye as a clubwoman amuses George because her clubs seem to plan most of their activities over cups of tea.

AND, I ALWAYS
ENJOY A
GOSSIP

32

...AND SO FOR WEEKS AND WEEKS IN FRONT OF THE LONG, MIRROR IN THEIR BEDROOM....

READY DEAR?

YES.... JUST **ONE** FINAL REHEARSAL

HOLD YOUR BREATH, DEAR

WAIT UNTIL MURIEL HEARS ABOUT THIS

WE SHOULD HAVE REHEARSED ON A **POLISHED** FLOOR— DEAR

51

I'D LOVE TO OWN A BOAT

COULDN'T AFFORD IT

TO GET AWAY FROM THE TRAFFIC... AWAY FROM ALL THE HUSTLE AND BUSTLE

115

NOW WE COME TO THE DIFFICULT JOB
OF CHOOSING A FEW OF THE LARGE
CARTOONS FROM THE SUNDAY EXPRESS

173

157

NEW NEIGHBOURS — GAYE COULD HARDLY WAIT TO MEET THEM!